This minibook of miracles

belongs to:

MAX LUCADO

HE STILL MOVES STONES

WORD PUBLISHING
Dallas · London · Vancouver · Melbourne

HE STILL MOVES STONES

Copyright © 1994 by Max Lucado.

Unless otherwise indicated, all Scripture quotations are from the New Century Version of the Bible, copyright © 1987, 1988, 1991, Word Publishing.

ISBN 0-8499-5072-4

3 4 5 6 9 PLP 9 8 7 6 5 4 3 2 1

Printed in Hong Kong

Chapter One

It's All Right to Dream Again

Facing Discouragement

The angel said to the women, "Don't be afraid. I know that you are looking for Jesus, who has been crucified. He is not here. He has risen from the dead as he said he would."

You know how you can read a
story you think you know and
then you read it again and see
something you've never seen?

Well, it happened to me.
Today.

Only God knows how many times I've read the resurrection story. At least a couple of dozen Easters and a couple of hundred times in between. But what I saw today I'd never seen before.

Mary and Mary knew a task had to be done—Jesus' body had to be prepared for burial. So early on that Sunday morning, they leave their pallets and walk out onto the tree-shadowed path. Theirs is a somber task. The morning promises only one encounter, an encounter with a corpse.

At that time there was a strong earthquake. An angel of the Lord came down from heaven, went to the tomb, and rolled the stone away from the entrance. Then he sat on the stone."

Why did the angel move the stone? For whom did he roll away the rock? For Jesus? That's what I always thought. I just assumed that the angel moved the stone so Jesus could come out.

But think about it. Did the stone have to be removed in order for Jesus to exit? Did God have to have help? Was the death conqueror so weak that he couldn't push away a rock? ("Hey, could somebody out there move this rock so I can get out?")

I don't think so. The text gives the impression that Jesus was already out when the stone was moved! Nowhere do the Gospels say that the angel moved the stone for Jesus. For whom, then, was the stone moved?

Listen to what the angel says:
"Come and see the place
where his body was."
The stone was moved—not for
Jesus but for the women; not
so Jesus could come out, but
so the women could see in!

Just when the road is too dark
for Mary and Mary, the angel
glows and the Savior shows
and the two women will never
be the same.

The lesson? Three words.
Don't give up.

Is the trail dark? Don't sit.

Is the road long? Don't stop.

Is the night black? Don't quit.

God is watching. For all you know right at this moment he may be telling the angel to move the stone.

God still sends angels. And God still moves stones.

Chapter Two

Not Guilty

Overcoming Shame

Then Jesus said, "I also don't judge you guilty."

That's her, the woman standing in the center of the circle. Those men around her are religious leaders. Pharisees, they are called. Self-appointed custodians of conduct. And the other man, the one in the simple clothes, the one sitting on the ground, the one looking at the face of the woman, that's Jesus.

Jesus has been teaching.
The woman has been cheating.
And the Pharisees are out to
stop them both.

Caught in the act of adultery."
The words alone are enough to
make you blush. Doors slammed
open. Covers jerked back.

"In the act." In the arms. In
the moment. In the embrace.

In an instant she is yanked from private passion to public spectacle. Clutching a thin robe around her shoulders, she hides her nakedness.

But nothing can hide her shame.

What the woman did is shameful, but what the Pharisees did is despicable. The evidence leaves little doubt. It was a trap. She's been caught. But she'll soon see that she is not the catch— she's only the bait.

The law of Moses commands that we stone to death every woman who does this. What do you say we should do?"

Pretty cocky, this committee
of high ethics. Pretty proud of
themselves, these agents of
righteousness. This will be a
moment they long remember,
the morning they foil and
snag the mighty Nazarene.

You'd expect Jesus to stand
and proclaim judgment on the
hypocrites. He doesn't. You'd
hope that he would snatch the
woman and the two would be
beamed to Galilee. That's not
what happens either.

Once again, his move is subtle.

But, once again, his message
is unmistakable.

What does Jesus do?

Jesus writes in the sand.

The same finger that engraved the commandments on Sinai's peak and seared the warning on Belshazzar's wall now scribbles in the courtyard floor. And as he writes, he speaks: "Anyone here who has never sinned can throw the first stone at her."

The young look to the old. The old look in their hearts. They are the first to drop their stones. And as they turn to leave, the young who were cocky with borrowed convictions do the same. The only sound is the thud of rocks and the shuffle of feet.

Jesus and the woman are left alone. "Woman, where are they? Has no one judged you guilty?"

She answers, "No one, sir."

Then Jesus says, "I also don't judge you guilty. You may go now, but don't sin anymore."

If you have ever wondered how God reacts when you fail, frame these words and hang them on the wall. Read them. Ponder them. Drink from them. Stand below them and let them wash over your soul.

And then listen. Listen carefully. He's speaking.

"I don't judge you guilty."

And watch. Watch carefully. He's writing. He's leaving a message. Not in the sand, but on a cross.

Not with his hand, but with his blood.

His message has two words:
Not guilty.

Chapter Three

Galilean Grace
When You Let God Down

The follower whom Jesus loved said to Peter, 'It is the Lord!' When Peter heard him say this, he wrapped his coat around himself. (Peter had taken his clothes off.) Then he jumped into the water.

What was I thinking?" Peter mumbled to himself as he stared at the bottom of the boat. *"Why did I run?"*

He had bragged, "Everyone else may stumble . . . but I will not." Yet he did. Peter did what he swore he wouldn't do. He had tumbled face first into the pit of his own fears. And there he sat.

He had turned his back on the sea to follow the Messiah. He had left the boats thinking he'd never return. But now he's back. Full circle. Same sea. Same boat. Maybe even the same spot.

But this isn't the same Peter.

Three years of living with the
Messiah have changed him.
He's seen too much. Too many
walking crippled, vacated graves,
too many hours hearing his
words. He's not the same
Peter. It's the same Galilee,
but a different fisherman.
Why did he return?

What brought him back to Galilee after the crucifixion? Despair? Some think so—I don't. Hope dies hard for a man who has known Jesus. I think that's what Peter has. That's what brought him back. Hope. A bizarre hope that on the sea where he knew him first, he would know him again.

His thoughts are interrupted
by a shout from the shore.
"Catch any fish?" Peter and
John look up. Probably a
villager. "No!" they yell. "Try
the other side!" the voice yells
back. John looks at Peter.
What harm? So out sails the
net. Peter wraps the rope
around his wrist to wait.

But there is no wait. The rope pulls taut and the net catches. Peter sets his weight against the side of the boat and begins to bring in the net; reaching down, pulling up, reaching down, pulling up. He's so intense with the task, he misses the message.

John doesn't. The moment is deja vu. This has happened before. The long night. The empty net. The call to cast again. Fish flapping on the floor of the boat. Wait a minute. He lifts his eyes to the man on the shore. "It's him," he whispers.

Then louder, "It's Jesus."

Then shouting, "It's the Lord,
Peter. It's the Lord!"

Peter turns and looks. Jesus
has come. Not just Jesus the
teacher, but Jesus the death-
defeater, Jesus the King . . .
Jesus the victor over darkness.
Jesus the God of heaven and
earth is on the shore . . .
and he's building a fire.

Peter plunges into the water, swims to the shore, and stumbles out wet and shivering and stands in front of the friend he betrayed.

Peter had failed God, but God had come to him.

For one of the few times in his life, Peter is silent. What words would suffice? The moment is too holy for words. God is offering breakfast to the friend who betrayed him. And Peter is once again finding grace at Galilee.

What do you say at a
moment like this?

What do *you* say at a
moment such as this?

It's just you and God. You and God both know what you did. And neither one of you is proud of it. What do you do?

You might consider doing what Peter did. Stand in God's presence. Stand in his sight. Stand still and wait. Sometimes that's all a soul can do. Too repentant to speak, but too hopeful to leave—we just stand.

Stand amazed.

He has come back.

He invites you to try again.
This time, with him.

Chapter Four

The Grave Fact

Understanding Death

After Jesus said this, he cried out in a loud voice, "Lazarus, come out!" The dead man came out, his hands and feet wrapped with pieces of cloth, and a cloth around his face.

Jesus said to them, "Take the cloth off of him and let him go."

She'd hoped Jesus would show
up to heal Lazarus. He didn't.
Then she'd hoped he'd show
up to bury Lazarus. He didn't.
By the time he made it to
Bethany, Lazarus was four-
days buried and Martha was
wondering what kind of friend
Jesus was.

She hears he's at the edge of town so she storms out to meet him. "Lord, if you had been here," she confronts, "my brother would not have died."

The funeral is over. The body is buried, and the grave is sealed.

And Martha is hurt.

Her words have been echoed in a thousand cemeteries. The grave unearths our view of God.

When we face death, our definition of God is challenged. Which, in turn, challenges our faith. Which leads me to ask a grave question. Why is it that we interpret the presence of death as the absence of God? Why do we think that if the body is not healed then God is not near?

Is healing the only way God demonstrates his presence? Sometimes we think so. And as a result, when God doesn't answer our prayers for healing, we get angry. Resentful. Blame replaces belief. "If you had been here, doing your part, God, then this death would not have happened."

It's distressing that this view
of God has no place for death.

Lazarus, come out!"

Martha was silent as Jesus commanded. The mourners were quiet. No one stirred as Jesus stood face to face with the rock-hewn tomb and demanded that it release his friend.

No one stirred, that is, except for Lazarus. Deep within the tomb, he moved. His stilled heart began to beat again. Wrapped eyes popped open. Wooden fingers lifted. And a mummied man in a tomb sat up. And want to know what happened next?

The dead man came out, his hands and feet wrapped with pieces of cloth, and a cloth around his face."

What's wrong with this picture? Dead men don't walk out of tombs.

What kind of God is this?

The God who holds the keys
to life and death.

The kind of God who rolls back the sleeve of the trickster and reveals death for the parlor trick it is.

The kind of God you want present at your funeral.

He'll do it again, you know. He's promised he would. And he's shown that he can.

"The Lord himself will come down from heaven with a loud command" (1 Thess. 4:16).

The same voice that awakened the corpse of Lazarus—the same voice will speak again. The earth and the sea will give up their dead. There will be no more death.

Jesus made sure of that.

There used to be a stone in front of a tomb. And it was moved. And I know that there are stones in your path. Stones that trip and stones that trap. Stones too big for you.

The God who spoke still speaks. The God who forgave still forgives. The God who came still comes. He comes into our world. He comes into your world. He comes to do what you can't. He comes to move the stones you can't budge.

Stones are no match for God.
Not then and not now.
He still moves stones.

Minibooks from Word

Angels Billy Graham

The Applause of Heaven Max Lucado

He Still Moves Stones Max Lucado

Laugh Again Charles Swindoll

On Raising Children
Mary Hollingsworth, compiler

Pack Up Your Gloomees Barbara Johnson

Peace with God Billy Graham

Silver Boxes Florence Littauer

Splashes of Joy in the Cesspools of Life
Barbara Johnson

Stick a Geranium in Your Hat and Be Happy
Barbara Johnson

Together Forever
Mary Hollingsworth, compiler

Unto the Hills Billy Graham